contents

savoury 2

sweet 18

glossary 60

conversion chart 62

index 63

NZ, Canada, US and UK readers
Please note that Australian cup and
spoon measurements are metric.
A conversion chart appears on page 62.

cottage pies

You need to purchase 48 baked 4cm tartlet cases for this recipe. They are available from most major supermarkets.

3 medium potatoes (600g), chopped coarsely
1 tablespoon olive oil
1 medium brown onion (150g), chopped finely
2 cloves garlic, crushed
250g beef mince
1 cup (250ml) tomato puree
⅓ cup (80ml) dry red wine
2 tablespoons worcestershire sauce
1 tablespoon fresh thyme leaves
¼ cup (30g) frozen peas
2 tablespoons finely chopped fresh flat-leaf parsley
¼ cup (60g) sour cream
1 egg yolk
48 x 4cm tartlet cases

1 Boil, steam or microwave potato until tender; drain.
2 Meanwhile, heat oil in large frying pan; cook onion and garlic, stirring, until onion softens. Add beef; cook, stirring, until beef changes colour. Stir in puree, wine, sauce and thyme; bring to a boil. Reduce heat; simmer, uncovered, about 15 minutes or until almost all liquid has evaporated. Stir in peas and parsley.
3 Mash potato in large bowl with sour cream and egg yolk. Spoon potato mixture into piping bag fitted with large fluted tube.
4 Meanwhile, preheat grill. Place pastry cases on oven trays. Divide beef mixture among cases; pipe potato over beef. Grill pies about 5 minutes or until tops brown and pies are heated through. Serve hot.

makes 48
preparation time 25 minutes
cooking time 30 minutes
per pie 2g fat; 164kJ (39 cal)

rocket, potato and bacon frittata

2 medium potatoes (400g)
2 bacon rashers (140g), chopped coarsely
1 medium brown onion (150g), chopped finely
1 clove garlic, crushed
50g baby rocket leaves, chopped coarsely
6 eggs, whisked lightly
¾ cup sour cream (180ml)

1 Preheat oven to 180°C/160°C fan-forced. Oil deep 20cm-round cake pan.

2 Boil, steam or microwave peeled whole potatoes until tender; cool, slice thinly.

3 Meanwhile cook bacon in small frying pan until browned. Add onion and garlic; cook, stirring, until onion is soft. Remove pan from heat; stir in rocket.

4 Place half the bacon mixture over base of pan; top with half the potato, remaining bacon mixture then remaining potato. Pour combined egg and sour cream carefully over bacon and potato; bake in oven about 35 minutes or until frittata is set and just cooked through.

5 If desired, brown top of frittata under hot grill. Stand cooked frittata 2 minutes before serving.

serves 4
preparation time 10 minutes
cooking time 50 minutes
per serving 29.2g fat; 1649kJ (394 cal)

caramelised onion and beetroot tart

50g butter
4 medium red onions (680g),
    halved, sliced thinly
1 tablespoon red wine vinegar
1 teaspoon fresh thyme leaves
3 medium beetroot
    (500g), trimmed
1 sheet ready-rolled puff pastry
cooking-oil spray
120g baby rocket leaves
chive oil
½ cup coarsely chopped
    fresh chives
¾ cup (180ml) olive oil
1 ice cube
horseradish cream
¾ cup (180ml) cream
1 tablespoon horseradish cream

1 Melt butter in medium frying pan; cook onion, stirring occasionally, over medium heat about 30 minutes or until caramelised. Stir in vinegar and thyme.

2 Meanwhile, boil, steam or microwave unpeeled beetroot until just tender; drain. When cool enough to handle, peel then slice beetroot thinly.

3 Preheat oven to 220°C/200°C fan-forced.

4 Cut 24cm circle out of pastry sheet. Place on oiled oven tray, prick all over with fork; freeze 10 minutes. Bake, uncovered, about 5 minutes or until browned lightly.

5 Make chive oil. Make horseradish cream.

6 Spread onion mixture over pastry; top with slightly overlapping beetroot slices. Spray tart lightly with oil; bake, uncovered, 10 minutes.

7 Meanwhile, combine rocket in medium bowl with half the chive oil; divide among serving plates.

8 Cut tart into six wedges. Place each wedge on rocket, drizzle with remaining chive oil; serve with horseradish cream.

chive oil Blend or process ingredients until smooth.

horseradish cream Beat cream in small bowl with electric mixer until soft peaks form; fold in horseradish cream.

serves 6
preparation time 20 minutes
cooking time 45 minutes
per serving 52.7g fat; 2436kJ (582 cal)

tomato tarte tatins
with crème fraîche sauce

9 small tomatoes (900g),
   peeled, quartered
30g butter
1 clove garlic, crushed
1 tablespoon brown sugar
2 tablespoons
   balsamic vinegar
1½ sheets ready-rolled
   puff pastry
1 egg, beaten lightly
vegetable oil, for deep-frying
6 sprigs fresh baby basil
crème fraîche sauce
20g butter
2 shallots (50g),
   chopped finely
1 cup (240g) crème fraîche
⅓ cup (80ml) water

1 Preheat oven to 200°C/180°C fan-forced.
2 Discard pulp and seeds from tomato; gently flatten flesh.
3 Melt butter in large frying pan; cook garlic, stirring, over low heat, until fragrant. Add sugar and vinegar; cook, stirring, until sugar dissolves. Place tomato, in single layer, in pan; cook, covered, turning once, about 5 minutes or until tomato softens.
4 Oil six 1-cup (250ml) metal pie dishes; cut six 11cm rounds from pastry sheets. Divide tomato among dishes; top each with a pastry round, pressing down gently. Brush pastry with egg; bake, uncovered, in oven about 15 minutes or until pastry is browned lightly and puffed.
5 Meanwhile, heat oil in small saucepan; using metal tongs, place thoroughly dry basil sprigs, one at a time, in pan. Deep-fry about 3 seconds or until basil is crisp. Drain.
6 Make crème fraîche sauce.
7 Divide sauce among serving plates; turn tarts onto sauce, top with basil.

crème fraîche sauce Melt butter in small saucepan; cook shallot, stirring, about 3 minutes or until softened. Add crème fraîche; cook, stirring, over low heat, until heated through. Stir in the water.

serves 6
preparation time 40 minutes
cooking time 30 minutes
per serving 33.4g fat; 1697kJ (405 cal)
tip Take care when deep-frying the basil sprigs as the hot oil is likely to splatter.

caramelised onion tart

3 cups (450g) plain flour
250g butter, chopped
2 egg yolks
¼ cup (60ml) cold water
50g butter, extra
2 large brown onions (400g),
    sliced thinly
2 cloves garlic, crushed
2 tablespoons brown sugar
1½ tablespoons
    balsamic vinegar
¼ cup (60ml) chicken stock
12 eggs, beaten lightly
¾ cup (180ml) cream
traditional pesto
1 clove garlic, quartered
1 cup firmly packed
    fresh basil leaves
¼ cup (40g) pine nuts, roasted
½ cup (40g) coarsely grated
    parmesan cheese
¼ cup (60ml) light olive oil

serves 8
preparation time 35 minutes
(plus refrigeration time)
cooking time 45 minutes
per serving 74.2g fat;
3889kJ (929 cal)

1 Process flour and butter until crumbly; add yolks and the water, process until ingredients just come together. Knead mixture gently on floured surface until smooth, wrap in plastic wrap; refrigerate dough 30 minutes.
2 Oil two 22cm round loose-based flan tins. Roll half the pastry between sheets of baking paper until large enough to line base and side of one tin. Lift pastry into tin, ease into side; trim edges. Repeat with remaining tin and pastry. Cover each tin with plastic wrap; refrigerate 30 minutes.
3 Preheat oven to 200°C/180°C fan-forced.
4 Discard plastic then cover pastry with baking paper; fill with dried beans. Place tins on oven trays; bake, uncovered, 10 minutes. Remove beans and paper, return tins to oven; bake, uncovered, about 10 minutes or until tart cases are browned lightly.
5 Meanwhile, melt extra butter in large frying pan; cook onion and garlic, stirring, until onion is soft. Add sugar, vinegar and stock; cook, stirring, about 15 minutes or until onion caramelises and liquid evaporates. Cool.
6 Reduce oven temperature to 160°C/140°C fan-forced. Divide onion mixture between tart cases; pour combined eggs and cream evenly over onion mixture.
7 Bake, uncovered, about 20 minutes or until filling is set. Serve tarts, hot or cooled, with pesto.

traditional pesto Blend or process garlic, basil, nuts and parmesan until combined. With motor operating, gradually pour in oil; process until a thick paste forms.

onion and anchovy tartlets

1 tablespoon olive oil
60g butter
3 medium brown onions (450g), halved, sliced thinly
2 cloves garlic, crushed
1 bay leaf
3 sprigs fresh thyme
⅓ cup coarsely chopped fresh flat-leaf parsley
8 drained anchovy fillets, chopped finely
2 tablespoons coarsely chopped seeded kalamata olives
¾ cup (110g) self-raising flour
¾ cup (110g) plain flour
¾ cup (180ml) buttermilk

1 Heat oil and half the butter in large frying pan; cook onion, garlic, bay leaf and thyme, stirring occasionally, about 20 minutes or until onion caramelises. Discard bay leaf and thyme; stir in parsley, anchovy and olives.
2 Meanwhile, blend or process flours and remaining butter until mixture resembles fine breadcrumbs. Add buttermilk; process until ingredients just come together. Knead dough on lightly floured surface until smooth.
3 Preheat oven to 200°C/180°C fan-forced. Oil two oven trays.
4 Divide dough into six pieces; roll each piece of dough on floured surface into 14cm square. Fold edges over to form 1cm border.
5 Place pastry squares on oven trays; place rounded tablespoons of the onion mixture on each square. Bake, uncovered, about 15 minutes or until pastry browns lightly.

serves 6
preparation time 45 minutes
cooking time 35 minutes
per serving 12.9g fat; 1184kJ (283 cal)

antipasto puff pastry tartlets

¼ cup (60ml) olive oil
2 cloves garlic, crushed
1 small red capsicum (150g), chopped coarsely
1 small yellow capsicum (150g), chopped coarsely
1 medium zucchini (120g), sliced thinly
2 baby eggplants (120g), sliced thinly
1 small red onion (100g), sliced thickly
100g semi-dried tomatoes
150g baby bocconcini cheese, halved
½ cup (40g) finely grated parmesan cheese
½ cup firmly packed fresh basil leaves
2 sheets ready-rolled puff pastry
⅓ cup (85g) bottled tomato pasta sauce
2 tablespoons bottled olive tapenade

1 Preheat oven to 200°C/180°C fan-forced.
2 Combine oil and garlic in large bowl. Add capsicums, zucchini, eggplant and onion; toss gently to coat vegetables in mixture.
3 Cook vegetables, in batches, on heated oiled grill plate (or grill or barbecue) until browned lightly and just tender; transfer to large bowl. Add tomatoes, cheeses and basil; toss gently to combine.
4 Cut pastry sheets in half; fold edges over to form 1cm border, place on oiled oven trays. Divide sauce among pastry pieces; top with vegetable mixture. Bake, uncovered, in oven about 15 minutes or until browned lightly. Serve tartlets topped with tapenade.

serves 4
preparation time 20 minutes
cooking time 20 minutes
per serving 29.8g fat; 1794kJ (429 cal)

creamy corn cake with salsa

1 egg yolk
½ cup (75g) self-raising flour
420g can corn kernels, rinsed, drained
310g can creamed corn
2 egg whites
avocado salsa
500g cherry tomatoes, quartered
1 small avocado (200g), chopped coarsely
1 small red onion (100g), chopped finely
2 tablespoons coarsely chopped fresh coriander
2 tablespoons coarsely chopped fresh mint
¼ cup (60ml) lime juice

1 Preheat oven to 220°C/200°C fan-forced. Oil deep 23cm-round cake pan; line base and side with baking paper.
2 Combine egg yolk, flour, corn kernels and creamed corn in medium bowl.
3 Beat egg whites in small bowl with electric mixer until soft peaks form; fold into corn mixture.
4 Spread mixture into pan; bake, uncovered, about 30 minutes or until browned lightly and cooked through.
5 Meanwhile, make salsa.
6 Cut cake into eight wedges; serve with avocado salsa.
avocado salsa Combine ingredients in small bowl; toss gently.

serves 8
preparation time 20 minutes
cooking time 30 minutes
per serving 5.5g fat; 677kJ (161 cal)

prune and custard tart

1½ cups (250g)
    seeded prunes
2 tablespoons brandy
300ml cream
3 eggs
⅔ cup (150g) caster sugar
1 teaspoon vanilla extract
pastry
1¼ cups (175g) plain flour
⅓ cup (55g) icing sugar
¼ cup (30g) almond meal
125g cold butter, chopped
1 egg yolk
1 tablespoon water

1 Make pastry.

2 Reduce oven temperature to 150°C/130°C fan-forced.

3 Blend or process prunes and brandy until mixture forms a paste; spread into tart shell.

4 Bring cream to a boil in small saucepan; remove from heat. Whisk eggs, sugar and extract in small bowl until combined; gradually add cream, whisking continuously until combined. Pour custard into tart shell; bake, uncovered, in oven about 20 minutes or until custard just sets. Stand 10 minutes; serve tart warm or cold dusted with icing sugar, if desired.

pastry Blend or process flour, icing sugar, meal and butter until mixture is crumbly. Add egg yolk and the water; process until ingredients just come together. Enclose in plastic wrap; refrigerate 30 minutes. Grease 26cm-round loose-based flan tin. Roll pastry between sheets of baking paper until large enough to line tin. Lift pastry into tin; press into side, trim edge. Prick base all over with fork. Cover; refrigerate 20 minutes. Preheat oven to 200°C/180°C fan-forced. Place tin on oven tray; cover pastry with baking paper, fill with dried beans or rice. Bake, uncovered, 10 minutes. Remove paper and beans carefully from tin; bake a further 5 minutes or until tart shell browns lightly. Cool to room temperature.

serves 8
preparation time 20 minutes
(plus refrigeration and cooling time)
cooking time 35 minutes
per serving 31.7g fat; 2275kJ (544 cal)

pear tarte tatin

3 large firm pears (990g)
90g butter, chopped
½ cup (110g) firmly packed brown sugar
⅔ cup (160ml) cream
¼ cup (30g) roasted pecans, chopped coarsely
pastry
1¼ cups (175g) plain flour
⅓ cup (55g) icing sugar
90g cold butter, chopped
1 egg yolk
1 tablespoon water

1 Peel and core pears; cut lengthways into quarters.
2 Melt butter with brown sugar in large frying pan. Add cream, stirring until sugar dissolves; bring to a boil. Add pear; reduce heat, simmer, turning occasionally, about 45 minutes or until tender.
3 Meanwhile, make pastry.
4 Preheat oven to 220°C/200°C fan-forced.
5 Place pear, round-side down, in deep 22cm-round cake pan; pour caramelised pan liquid over pear, sprinkle with nuts.
6 Roll pastry between sheets of baking paper until slightly larger than pan. Remove top paper, turn pastry onto pears. Remove remaining paper; tuck pastry between pears and side of pan. Bake, uncovered, in oven about 25 minutes or until pastry is browned lightly. Cool 5 minutes; turn tart onto serving plate. Serve with cinnamon-scented whipped cream, if desired.
pastry Blend or process flour, icing sugar and butter until mixture is crumbly. Add egg yolk and the water; process until ingredients just come together. Enclose in plastic wrap; refrigerate 30 minutes.

serves 6
preparation time 20 minutes (plus refrigeration time)
cooking time 1 hour 15 minutes
per serving 40.7g fat; 2690kJ (643 cal)

lime meringue tartlets

2 eggs, separated
2 tablespoons caster sugar
1 teaspoon finely grated lime rind
1½ tablespoons lime juice
20g butter
20 x 4cm pastry shells
½ cup (110g) caster sugar, extra
⅔ cup (50g) shredded coconut

1 Combine egg yolks, sugar, rind, juice and butter in small heatproof bowl. Stir constantly over small saucepan of simmering water until mixture thickens slightly and coats the back of a spoon; remove from heat. Cover; refrigerate curd until cold.
2 Preheat oven to 220°C/200°C fan-forced.
3 Divide curd evenly among pastry shells.
4 Beat egg whites in small bowl with electric mixer until soft peaks form; gradually add extra sugar, 1 tablespoon at a time, beating until sugar dissolves between additions. Gently fold in ½ cup of the coconut.
5 Spoon meringue evenly over curd. Sprinkle remaining coconut over meringue; bake about 5 minutes or until meringue is browned lightly. Refrigerate until ready to serve.

makes 20
preparation time 25 minutes (plus refrigeration time)
cooking time 15 minutes
per tartlet 6g fat; 460kJ (110 cal)
tip Pastry shells are made from shortcrust pastry and can be found at some supermarkets. They may be frozen in an airtight container.

chocolate butterscotch tartlets

12 frozen tartlet cases
¼ cup (55g) firmly packed brown sugar
20g butter
¼ cup (60ml) cream
150g dark eating chocolate, chopped coarsely
¼ cup (60ml) cream, extra
2 tablespoons coarsely chopped roasted hazelnuts
1 tablespoon cocoa powder

1 Bake tartlet cases according to manufacturer's instructions.
2 Meanwhile, heat sugar, butter and cream in small saucepan, stirring until sugar dissolves. Reduce heat; simmer, uncovered, without stirring, 2 minutes. Cool 5 minutes. Stir in chocolate and extra cream; refrigerate 10 minutes.
3 Divide mixture among tartlet cases, sprinkle with nuts and sifted cocoa.

makes 12
preparation time 5 minutes
cooking time 10 minutes
per tartlet 38.8g fat; 2352kJ (562 cal)

SWEET

lime meringue pie

250g plain sweet biscuits
100g unsalted butter, melted
½ cup (75g) wheaten cornflour
1½ cups (330g) caster sugar
½ cup (125ml) lime juice
1¼ cups (310ml) water
60g unsalted butter, extra
4 eggs, separated
2 teaspoons finely grated
   lime rind

1 Grease 24cm-round loose-based flan tin.
2 Blend or process biscuits until mixture resembles fine breadcrumbs. Add butter; process until combined.
3 Press biscuit mixture evenly over base and 2cm up the side of tin, place on oven tray; refrigerate while preparing filling.
4 Combine cornflour and ½ cup of the sugar in medium saucepan; gradually stir in juice and the water until smooth. Cook, stirring, over high heat until mixture boils and thickens. Reduce heat; simmer, stirring, 1 minute. Remove from heat; stir in extra butter then yolks and rind. Continue stirring until butter melts. Cool 10 minutes.
5 Spread filling over biscuit base, cover; refrigerate 2 hours.
6 Preheat oven to 200°C/180°C fan-forced.
7 Beat egg whites in small bowl with electric mixer until soft peaks form; add remaining sugar, 1 tablespoon at a time, beating until sugar dissolves between additions.
8 Roughen surface of filling with a fork before spreading with meringue mixture. Bake, uncovered, about 5 minutes or until meringue is browned lightly.

serves 10
preparation time 15 minutes
(plus refrigeration time)
cooking time 15 minutes
per serving 19.5g fat; 1781kJ (426 cal)

rich chocolate tart

4 egg yolks

2 eggs

¼ cup (55g) caster sugar

⅓ cup (80ml) thickened cream

300g dark eating
   chocolate, melted

1 teaspoon vanilla extract

pastry

1¼ cups (185g) plain flour

¼ cup (25g) cocoa powder

⅓ cup (55g) icing sugar

150g cold butter, chopped

2 egg yolks

1 teaspoon iced water

1 Make pastry. Reduce oven temperature to 160°C/140°C fan-forced.

2 Beat egg yolks, whole eggs and sugar in small bowl with electric mixer until thick and creamy. Fold in cream, chocolate and extract.

3 Pour chocolate mixture into pastry case. Bake, uncovered, about 30 minutes or until filling is set. Cool 10 minutes.

4 Serve tart dusted with a little extra sifted cocoa, if desired.

pastry Blend or process flour, cocoa, icing sugar and butter until combined. Add egg yolks and the water; process until ingredients just come together. Knead dough on floured surface until smooth. Cover with plastic wrap; refrigerate 30 minutes. Roll dough between two sheets of baking paper until large enough to line base and side of greased 24cm-round loose-based flan tin. Ease dough into tin, press into side; trim edge. Cover; refrigerate 30 minutes. Preheat oven to 180°C/160°C fan-forced. Cover pastry case with baking paper, fill with dried beans or rice; place on oven tray. Bake, uncovered, 15 minutes. Remove paper and beans; bake, uncovered, 10 minutes or until browned lightly. Cool.

serves 10

preparation time 25 minutes
(plus refrigeration time)

cooking time 55 minutes

per serving 30.5g fat; 2098kJ (502 cal)

29

pecan pie

2 cups (240g) roasted pecans
6 egg yolks
½ cup (175g) golden syrup
½ cup (110g) firmly packed
   brown sugar
90g butter, melted
¼ cup (60ml) thickened cream
pastry
1¼ cups (185g) plain flour
⅓ cup (55g) icing sugar
125g cold butter, chopped
1 egg yolk
1 teaspoon lemon juice

1 Make pastry.
2 Place nuts in pastry case. Combine egg yolks, syrup, sugar, butter and cream in small bowl; whisk until smooth. Pour mixture over nuts; bake, uncovered, about 30 minutes or until set. Cool. Serve with cream, if desired.

pastry Blend or process flour, icing sugar and butter until combined. Add egg yolks and juice; process until ingredients just come together. Knead dough on floured surface until smooth. Cover; refrigerate 30 minutes. Grease 24cm-round loose-based flan tin. Roll dough between two sheets of baking paper until large enough to line tin. Ease dough into tin, press into side; trim edge. Cover; refrigerate 30 minutes. Preheat oven to 180°C/160°C fan-forced. Place tin on oven tray. Line pastry case with baking paper, fill with dried beans or rice. Bake, uncovered, 15 minutes. Remove paper and beans; bake, uncovered, a further 5 minutes or until browned lightly.

serves 8
preparation time 25 minutes
(plus refrigeration time)
cooking time 50 minutes
per serving 48.8g fat; 2905kJ (695 cal)
tip Uncooked rice or dried beans used to weigh down the pastry are not suitable for eating. Use them every time you bake blind; cool, then store in an airtight jar.

roast nectarine tart

8 nectarines (1.5kg), halved,
  stones removed
¼ cup (60ml) orange juice
½ cup (110g) firmly packed
  brown sugar
pastry
1⅔ cups (250g) plain flour
⅔ cup (110g) icing sugar
125g cold butter, chopped
1 egg yolk
1½ tablespoons cold water,
  approximately
crème pâtissière
300ml thickened cream
1 cup (250ml) milk
½ cup (110g) caster sugar
1 vanilla bean
3 egg yolks
2 tablespoons cornflour
90g unsalted butter, chopped

serves 8
preparation time 40 minutes
(plus refrigeration and
cooling time)
cooking time 45 minutes
per serving 40.7g fat;
2847kJ (681 cal)

1 Make pastry. Make crème pâtissière while pastry case is cooling.

2 Increase oven temperature to 220°C/200°C fan-forced.

3 Place nectarines in large shallow baking dish; sprinkle with juice and sugar. Roast about 20 minutes or until nectarines are soft. Cool.

4 Meanwhile, spoon crème pâtissière into pastry case, cover; refrigerate about 30 minutes or until firm. Top with nectarines.

pastry Process flour, icing sugar and butter until combined. Add yolk and enough water to make ingredients just come together. Knead dough on floured surface until smooth. Cover; refrigerate 30 minutes. Grease 19cm x 27cm loose-based flan tin. Roll dough between sheets of baking paper until large enough to line tin. Ease dough into tin, press into sides; trim edges. Cover; refrigerate 30 minutes. Preheat oven to 180°C/160°C fan-forced. Cover pastry case with baking paper, fill with dried beans; place on oven tray. Bake 10 minutes. Remove paper and beans; bake a further 10 minutes or until pastry case is browned lightly. Cool.

crème pâtissière Combine cream, milk and sugar in saucepan. Split vanilla bean in half lengthways, scrape seeds into saucepan then add pod; bring to a boil. Remove from heat; discard pod. Beat yolks in small bowl with electric mixer until thick and creamy; beat in cornflour. Gradually beat in hot cream mixture. Strain mixture into same cleaned saucepan; stir over heat until mixture boils and thickens. Remove from heat; whisk in butter. Cover surface with plastic wrap; cool to room temperature.

33

blackberry and apple pie

9 medium apples (1.4kg)
2 tablespoons caster sugar
1 tablespoon cornflour
1 tablespoon water
300g frozen blackberries
1 tablespoon cornflour, extra
1 tablespoon demerara sugar
pastry
2 cups (300g) plain flour
⅔ cup (110g) icing sugar
185g cold butter, chopped
2 egg yolks
1 tablespoon iced water,
   approximately

serves 8
preparation time 50 minutes
(plus refrigeration time)
cooking time 1 hour
per serving 21.1g fat;
2031kJ (486 cal)
tips We used golden
delicious apples in this recipe.
For a different flavour, replace
blackberries with blueberries,
raspberries or strawberries.

1 Peel and core apples; slice thinly. Place in saucepan with caster sugar; cook, covered, over low heat, 10 minutes or until apples are just tender. Strain over small saucepan; reserve cooking liquid. Blend cornflour with the water, stir into reserved cooking liquid over heat until mixture boils and thickens. Place apples in large bowl, gently stir in cornflour mixture.
2 Meanwhile, make pastry.
3 Toss blackberries in extra cornflour; stir gently into apple mixture.
4 Preheat oven to 220°C/200°C fan-forced.
5 Spoon fruit mixture into pastry case; top with remaining pastry. Press edges together, trim. Brush pastry with a little water; sprinkle with demerara sugar. Make three cuts in top of pastry to allow steam to escape. Place pie on oven tray; bake, uncovered, 20 minutes.
6 Reduce oven temperature to 200°C/180°C fan-forced; bake a further 30 minutes or until pastry is browned lightly. Stand 10 minutes before serving.

pastry Blend or process flour, icing sugar and butter until combined. Add egg yolks and enough of the water to make ingredients just come together. Knead dough on floured surface until smooth. Refrigerate 30 minutes. Roll two-thirds of the dough between sheets of baking paper until large enough to line greased 23cm pie dish. Ease dough into dish; trim edge. Cover; refrigerate 30 minutes. Roll remaining pastry between sheets of baking paper until large enough to cover pie.

tarte tatin

6 large apples (1.2kg)
100g unsalted butter, chopped
1 cup (220g) firmly packed brown sugar
2 tablespoons lemon juice
pastry
1 cup (150g) plain flour
2 tablespoons caster sugar
80g cold unsalted butter, chopped
2 tablespoons sour cream

1 Peel, core and quarter apples. Melt butter in large heavy-based frying pan; add apple, sprinkle evenly with sugar and juice. Cook, uncovered, over low heat, 1 hour, turning apple as it caramelises.

2 Place apple, rounded-sides down, in 23cm pie dish; drizzle with 1 tablespoon of the caramel mixture. Reserve remaining caramel. Pack apple tightly to avoid any gaps, cover; refrigerate while preparing pastry.

3 Make pastry.

4 Preheat oven to 200°C/180°C fan-forced.

5 Roll dough between sheets of baking paper until large enough to cover apple. Peel away one sheet of baking paper; invert pastry over apple. Remove remaining paper; tuck pastry around apple. Bake, uncovered, about 30 minutes or until browned. Carefully turn onto serving plate.

6 Reheat reserved caramel over low heat; drizzle over apple.

pastry Blend or process ingredients until they just come together. Knead dough on floured surface until smooth. Cover; refrigerate 30 minutes.

serves 8
preparation time 40 minutes (plus refrigeration time)
cooking time 1 hour 45 minutes
per serving 20.9g fat; 1818kJ (435 cal)
tip You may need to use a simmer mat or cover the pan occasionally while the apple is caramelising to prevent the evaporation of too much liquid and subsequent burning.

peanut butter and fudge ice-cream pie

300g packet chocolate chip cookies
40g butter, melted
1 tablespoon milk
1 litre vanilla ice-cream
1⅓ cups (375g) crunchy peanut butter
hot fudge sauce
200g dark eating chocolate, chopped coarsely
50g large white marshmallows, chopped coarsely
300ml thickened cream

1 Grease 24cm-round loose-based flan tin.
2 Blend or process cookies until mixture resembles coarse breadcrumbs. Add butter and milk; process until combined.
3 Press cookie mixture evenly over base and around side of tin; refrigerate 10 minutes.
4 Beat softened ice-cream and peanut butter in large bowl with electric mixer until combined; spoon into crumb crust. Cover; freeze pie 3 hours or overnight.
5 Meanwhile, make hot fudge sauce.
6 Drizzle slices of pie with hot fudge sauce to serve.
hot fudge sauce Combine ingredients in small saucepan; stir over heat, without boiling, until smooth.

serves 10
preparation time 20 minutes (plus freezing time)
cooking time 10 minutes
per serving 52g fat; 3068kJ (734 cal)

lime macaroon tart

1 cup (150g) plain flour
¼ cup (40g) icing sugar
100g cold butter, chopped
1 egg yolk
1 teaspoon iced water
lime filling
2 teaspoons finely grated
   lime rind
¼ cup (60ml) lime juice
4 eggs
⅓ cup (75g) white sugar
1 cup (250ml) cream
macaroon topping
2 egg whites
½ cup (110g) white sugar
½ cup (40g) shredded
   coconut, toasted

1 Process flour, icing sugar, butter, yolk and the water until ingredients just come together. Knead dough on floured surface until smooth. Cover; refrigerate 30 minutes.

2 Grease 11cm x 35cm rectangular, or 20cm-round, loose-based flan tin. Roll pastry between two sheets of baking paper until large enough to line tin; lift pastry into tin. Ease into sides; trim edges. Cover; refrigerate 30 minutes.

3 Preheat oven to 200°C/180°C fan-forced.

4 Cover pastry with baking paper; fill with dried beans or rice. Place tin on oven tray; bake 15 minutes. Remove paper and beans; bake, uncovered, 10 minutes or until pastry is browned lightly. Cool; refrigerate until cold. Reduce oven temperature to 160°C/140°C fan-forced.

5 Meanwhile, make lime filling. Pour filling into pastry case. Bake, uncovered, about 30 minutes or until filling has set slightly; cool.

6 Make macaroon topping. Preheat grill. Spread macaroon topping evenly over tart; cook under hot grill until browned lightly.

lime filling Whisk ingredients in medium bowl. Stand 5 minutes; strain.

macaroon topping Beat egg whites in small bowl with electric mixer until soft peaks form. Gradually add sugar, in batches, beating until dissolved between additions; fold in coconut.

serves 6
preparation time 30 minutes
(plus refrigeration time)
cooking time 1 hour
per serving 40.1g fat; 2604kJ (622 cal)

chocolate jaffa tart

3 eggs
1 tablespoon finely grated
orange rind
⅔ cup (160ml)
thickened cream
¾ cup (165g) caster sugar
60g dark eating
chocolate, melted
2 tablespoons cocoa powder
2 tablespoons Grand Marnier
140g dark eating chocolate,
chopped coarsely, extra
¼ cup (60ml) thickened
cream, extra
20 Ferrero Rocher
chocolates, halved
pastry
1½ cups (225g) plain flour
¼ cup (40g) icing sugar
125g cold unsalted
butter, chopped
2 egg yolks
2 teaspoons iced water,
approximately

1 Make pastry.
2 Meanwhile, whisk eggs, rind, cream, sugar, chocolate, sifted cocoa powder and liqueur in medium bowl until combined.
3 Pour chocolate mixture into pastry case. Bake about 30 minutes or until filling is set; cool.
4 Place extra chocolate and extra cream in small saucepan; stir over low heat until smooth. Spread warm chocolate mixture over top of cold tart; refrigerate until set. Just before serving, decorate with Ferrero Rocher halves.
pastry Blend or process flour, icing sugar and butter until crumbly. Add egg yolks and enough of the water to make ingredients just come together. Knead pastry on floured surface until smooth. Cover with plastic wrap; refrigerate 30 minutes. Grease 24cm-round loose-based flan tin. Roll pastry between two sheets of baking paper until large enough to line tin; lift pastry into tin. Press into side; trim edge. Cover; refrigerate 30 minutes. Preheat oven to 200°C/180°C fan-forced. Cover pastry with baking paper; fill with dried beans or rice. Place tin on oven tray; bake 10 minutes. Remove paper and beans. Bake a further 10 minutes or until pastry is browned lightly; cool. Reduce oven temperature to 180°C/160°C fan-forced.

serves 8
preparation time 30 minutes
(plus refrigeration and cooling time)
cooking time 55 minutes
per serving 47.1g fat; 3302kJ (790 cal)

mini pecan, macadamia and walnut pies

1¼ cups (185g) plain flour
⅓ cup (55g) icing sugar
¼ cup (30g) almond meal
125g cold butter, chopped
1 egg yolk
filling
⅓ cup (45g) roasted
   macadamias
⅓ cup (40g) roasted pecans
⅓ cup (35g) roasted walnuts
2 tablespoons brown sugar
1 tablespoon plain flour
40g butter, melted
2 eggs, beaten lightly
¾ cup (180ml) maple syrup

1 Blend or process flour, icing sugar and meal with butter until combined. Add egg yolk; process until ingredients just come together. Knead pastry on floured surface until smooth. Cover with plastic wrap; refrigerate 30 minutes.
2 Grease four 10cm-round loose-based flan tins. Divide pastry into quarters. Roll each piece between two sheets of baking paper into rounds large enough to line tins; lift pastry into each tin. Press into sides; trim edges. Cover; refrigerate 1 hour.
3 Preheat oven to 200°C/180°C fan-forced.
4 Place tins on oven tray, cover each with baking paper; fill with dried beans or rice. Bake 10 minutes; remove paper and beans. Bake a further 7 minutes or until pastry cases are browned lightly; cool.
5 Meanwhile, make filling.
6 Reduce oven temperature to 180°C/160°C fan-forced. Divide filling among cases. Bake about 25 minutes or until set; cool.
filling Combine ingredients in medium bowl; mix well.

makes 4
preparation time 20 minutes
(plus refrigeration time)
cooking time 25 minutes
per pie 64.5g fat; 4318kJ (1033 cal)

caramel chocolate tarts

1 cup (150g) plain flour
90g cold butter, chopped
¼ cup (55g) caster sugar
395g can sweetened condensed milk
30g butter, extra
2 tablespoons golden syrup
100g dark eating chocolate, melted

1 Preheat oven to 180°C/160°C fan-forced. Grease two 12-hole mini-muffin pans (1½-tablespoon/30ml).

2 Blend or process flour, butter and sugar until ingredients just come together. Press level tablespoons of mixture into pan holes. Bake about 10 minutes or until browned lightly.

3 Meanwhile, combine condensed milk, extra butter and syrup in small saucepan; stir until smooth. Do not boil.

4 Pour hot caramel filling over hot bases; return to oven about 3 minutes or until caramel begins to brown around the edges. Stand 2 minutes. Using a pointed vegetable knife, gently remove tarts from pans. Cool.

5 Spread top of cooled tarts with melted chocolate; stand until set.

makes 24
preparation time 25 minutes (plus cooling and standing time)
cooking time 15 minutes
per tart 6.9g fat; 627kJ (149 cal)

chocolate ricotta tart

¼ cup (35g) white
  self-raising flour
¼ cup (40g) wholemeal
  self-raising flour
2 tablespoons caster sugar
2 teaspoons cocoa powder
30g low-fat dairy-free spread
1 egg yolk
2 teaspoons water
ricotta filling
150g low-fat ricotta cheese
1 egg
1 egg yolk
¼ cup (70g) low-fat yogurt
¼ cup (55g) caster sugar
2 teaspoons white plain flour
2 tablespoons dark Choc Bits
2 teaspoons coffee-flavoured
  liqueur

1 Process flours, sugar, cocoa and spread until crumbly; add egg yolk and the water, process until ingredients just cling together. Knead dough gently on lightly floured surface until smooth, cover; refrigerate 30 minutes.
2 Preheat oven to 200°C/180°C fan-forced.
3 Grease 18cm-round loose-based flan tin. Roll pastry between two sheets of baking paper until large enough to line tin. Ease pastry into tin; trim edges. Cover; refrigerate 30 minutes. Cover pastry with baking paper, fill with dried beans or rice; place tin on oven tray. Bake 10 minutes, remove beans and paper. Bake a further 5 minutes or until pastry is browned lightly; cool. Reduce oven temperature to 180°C/160°C fan-forced.
4 Meanwhile, make ricotta filling.
5 Pour ricotta filling into tin; bake, uncovered, about 20 minutes. Cool; refrigerate until firm.
ricotta filling Using electric mixer, beat ricotta, egg, egg yolk, yogurt, sugar and flour in medium bowl until smooth. Stir in Choc Bits and liqueur.

serves 8
preparation time 15 minutes
(plus refrigeration time)
cooking time 35 minutes
per serving 6.5g fat; 706kJ (169 cal)

caramelised apple tart

4 small apples (520g)
50g butter
¼ cup (55g) firmly packed brown sugar
½ teaspoon ground cinnamon
½ cup (60g) pecans
¼ cup (75g) apple sauce
2 teaspoons lemon juice
2 sheets ready-rolled puff pastry
1 egg, beaten lightly

1 Peel and core apples; slice thinly. Stir butter, sugar and cinnamon in medium saucepan over low heat until sugar dissolves; add apple. Cook, stirring occasionally, over low heat, until apple softens. Drain apple mixture over medium bowl; reserve caramel mixture.
2 Meanwhile, blend or process pecans, apple sauce and juice until smooth.
3 Preheat oven to 200°C/180°C fan-forced. Line oven tray with baking paper.
4 Cut eight 11cm rounds from pastry sheets; place four of the rounds on tray; brush with egg. Using 9cm cutter, remove and discard centres from four remaining rounds; centre pastry rings on top of the 11cm rounds.
5 Spread pecan mixture in centre of rounds; top with apple mixture. Bake tarts, uncovered, about 15 minutes or until golden brown. Serve warm, with heated reserved caramel mixture.

makes 4
preparation time 10 minutes
cooking time 20 minutes
per tart 39.7g fat; 2606kJ (623 cal)

rhubarb galette

You need about four trimmed large stems of rhubarb for this recipe.

20g butter, melted
2½ cups (275g) coarsely chopped rhubarb
⅓ cup (75g) firmly packed brown sugar
1 teaspoon finely grated orange rind
1 sheet ready-rolled puff pastry
2 tablespoons almond meal
10g butter, melted, extra

1 Preheat oven to 220°C/200°C fan-forced. Line oven tray with baking paper.
2 Combine butter, rhubarb, sugar and rind in medium bowl.
3 Cut 24cm round from pastry, place on tray; sprinkle meal evenly over pastry. Spread rhubarb mixture over pastry, leaving a 4cm border. Fold 2cm of pastry edge up and around filling. Brush edge with extra butter.
4 Bake galette, uncovered, about 20 minutes or until browned lightly.

serves 4
preparation time 10 minutes
cooking time 20 minutes
per serving 18.2g fat; 1326kJ (317 cal)

lemon tart

1¼ cups (185g) plain flour
⅓ cup (55g) icing sugar
¼ cup (30g) almond meal
125g cold butter, chopped
1 egg yolk
lemon filling
1 tablespoon finely grated lemon rind
½ cup (125ml) lemon juice
5 eggs
¾ cup (165g) caster sugar
300ml thickened cream

1 Process flour, icing sugar, meal and butter until combined. Add egg yolk; process until ingredients just come together. Knead dough on floured surface until smooth. Cover; refrigerate 30 minutes.
2 Grease 24cm round loose-based flan tin. Roll pastry between two sheets of baking paper until large enough to line tin. Ease pastry into tin; trim edges. Cover; refrigerate 30 minutes.
3 Preheat oven to 200°C/180°C fan-forced.
4 Cover pastry with baking paper, fill with dried beans or rice; place tin on oven tray. Bake 10 minutes. Remove beans and paper; bake about 10 minutes or until browned lightly, cool to room temperature.
5 Reduce oven temperature to 160°C/140°C fan-forced.
6 Meanwhile, make lemon filling. Pour lemon filling into pastry case. Bake, uncovered, about 40 minutes or until filling just sets. Stand 10 minutes; refrigerate lemon tart until cold.
lemon filling Whisk ingredients in medium bowl. Stand 5 minutes; strain.

serves 8
preparation time 20 minutes (plus refrigeration and cooling time)
cooking time 1 hour 10 minutes
per serving 33g fat; 2133kJ (509 cal)

peach galette

2 medium peaches (300g)
6 sheets fillo pastry
60g butter, melted
3 teaspoons white sugar
1 tablespoon apricot jam, warmed, sieved

1 Preheat oven to 200°C/180°C fan-forced. Line oven tray with baking paper.
2 Halve peaches, discard seeds; slice peach halves thinly.
3 Place two pastry sheets on board; brush lightly with a third of the butter. Top with two more pastry sheets; brush lightly with half of the remaining butter. Repeat layering with remaining pastry and butter.
4 Fold pastry in half to form a square; cut 22cm-diameter circle from pastry square. Arrange peach slices on pastry circle; sprinkle with sugar. Bake about 20 minutes or until galette is browned lightly.
5 Brush galette with jam; serve warm.

serves 4
preparation time 15 minutes
cooking time 20 minutes
per serving 13g fat; 991kJ (237 cal)
tips Cover the pastry with greaseproof paper then a damp towel when you're working with it, to prevent it drying out. Nectarines, apricots, apples, plums and pears are all suitable to use in place of the peaches.

chocolate cases with mascarpone and berries

We used Grand Marnier in this recipe, but you can use Cointreau or any other orange-flavoured liqueur, if you prefer. You need a small, unused paintbrush for this recipe. Paper cases can be found in confectionery stores and some supermarkets.

16 x 2.5cm paper cases
cooking-oil spray
100g dark chocolate Melts, melted
½ cup (140g) mascarpone cheese
1 tablespoon orange-flavoured liqueur
100g fresh raspberries
100g fresh blueberries

1 Lightly spray paper cases with cooking-oil spray. Using small, new, cleaned brush, paint chocolate thickly on inside of each case. Place paper cases on tray; refrigerate about 5 minutes or until chocolate sets. Peel away and discard paper cases.
2 Meanwhile, combine mascarpone and liqueur in small bowl. Place 1 teaspoon of the mascarpone mixture in each chocolate case; top with berries. Sprinkle with sifted icing sugar, if desired.

makes 16
preparation time 30 minutes (plus refrigeration time)
per case 7.1g fat; 380kJ (91 cal)

glossary

almond meal also known as ground almonds; nuts are powdered to a coarse flour-like texture.

bacon rashers also known as bacon slices.

basil an aromatic herb; there are many types, but the most commonly used is sweet, or common basil.

beetroot also known as red beets or beets.

butter use salted or unsalted (sweet) butter; 125g is equal to one stick of butter.

buttermilk sold alongside fresh milk products in supermarkets; originally the liquid left after cream was separated from milk, today, it is commercially made similarly to yogurt.

capsicum also known as bell pepper or pepper; can be red, green, yellow, orange or purplish black. Seeds and membranes should be discarded before use.

cheese

bocconcini walnut-sized, baby mozzarella, a delicate, semi-soft, white cheese.

mascarpone a buttery-rich, cream-like cheese made from cow milk. Ivory-coloured, soft and delicate, with the texture of softened butter.

parmesan also known as parmigiano; a hard, grainy cow-milk cheese.

ricotta a soft, white, cow-milk cheese with a sweet, moist flavour.

chocolate

choc bits also known as chocolate chips and chocolate morsels. Hold their shape in baking and are ideal for decorating.

dark eating made of cocoa liquor, cocoa butter and sugar.

dark Melts discs of dark compounded chocolate ideal for melting.

cinnamon dried inner bark of the shoots of the cinnamon tree; available in stick or ground form.

cocoa powder also known as cocoa; dried, roasted, unsweetened, ground cocoa beans.

coconut, shredded thin strips of dried coconut.

coriander also known as cilantro or chinese parsley; bright-green leafy herb with a pungent flavour.

cornflour also known as cornstarch.

cream

thickened a whipping cream containing a thickener.

sour a thick commercially-cultured soured cream.

crème fraîche a mature, naturally fermented cream with a velvety texture and slightly tangy, nutty flavour.

dairy-free spread a dairy-free margarine product.

egg some recipes in this book may call for raw or barely cooked eggs; exercise caution if there is a salmonella problem in your area.

eggplant also known as aubergine. Ranging in size from tiny to very large, and in colour from pale-green to deep-purple.

flour

plain an all-purpose flour, made from wheat.

self-raising plain flour sifted with baking powder in the proportion of 1 cup flour to 2 teaspoons baking powder.

golden syrup a by-product of refined sugarcane; pure maple syrup or honey can be substituted.

Grand Marnier an orange-flavoured liqueur.

hazelnuts also known as filberts; plump, grape-size, rich, sweet nut having a brown inedible skin that is removed by rubbing heated nuts together vigorously in a tea towel.

horseradish cream a creamy prepared paste of grated horseradish, vinegar, oil and sugar.

jam also known as preserve or conserve.

macadamias a rich, buttery nut native to Australia; store in the refrigerator because of its high oil content.

maple syrup a thin syrup distilled from the sap of the maple tree. Maple-flavoured syrup or pancake syrup is not an adequate substitute for the real thing.

mince also known as ground meat.

nashi also called Japanese or Asian pear; a member of the pear family but similar in appearance to an apple.

nectarines smooth-skinned, slightly smaller cousin to the peach; juicy, with a rich and rather spicy flavour.

oil

cooking-oil spray we use a cholesterol-free cooking spray made from canola oil.

olive made from ripened olives. *Extra virgin* and *virgin* are the best, while *extra light* or *light* refers to taste not fat levels.

vegetable any of a number of oils sourced from plants rather than animal fats.

olive tapenade a thick paste made from black or green olives, capers, anchovies, olive oil and lemon juice.

onion, red also known as spanish, red spanish or bermuda onion; a large, sweet-flavoured, purple-red onion.

parsley flat-leaf also known as continental or Italian parsley.

pastry

fillo also known as phyllo; tissue-thin pastry sheets purchased chilled or frozen.

ready-rolled puff packaged sheets of frozen puff pastry, available from supermarkets.

pine nuts also known as pignoli; not a nut but a small, cream-coloured kernel from pine cones.

prunes dried plums.

rocket also known as rugula, arugula and rucola; a green, peppery-tasting leaf.

shallots also called french shallots, golden shallots or eschalots.

stock available in tetra packs, cans or bottles. Stock cubes or powder can be used.

sugar

brown soft, finely granulated sugar retaining molasses for its colour and flavour.

caster also known as superfine or finely granulated table sugar.

demerara small grain golden-coloured sugar.

sugar icing also known as confectioners' sugar or powdered sugar; granulated sugar crushed together with a small amount of cornflour.

white coarse, granulated table sugar, also known as crystal sugar.

sweetened condensed milk milk from which 60% of the water has been removed; the remaining milk is then sweetened with sugar.

thyme a member of the mint family; has tiny grey-green leaves that have a pungent minty, light-lemon aroma.

tomato

cherry also known as tiny tim or tom thumb tomatoes; small and round.

egg also called plum or roma; smallish, oval tomatoes.

pasta sauce a blend of tomatoes, herbs and spices.

puree canned pureed tomatoes (not tomato paste). Substitute with fresh peeled and pureed tomatoes.

semi-dried partially dried tomatoes in oil; softer and juicier than sun-dried.

vanilla

bean dried, long, thin pod from a tropical golden orchid grown in central and South America and Tahiti; the tiny black seeds inside the bean are used to impart a luscious vanilla flavour.

extract obtained from vanilla beans infused in water; a non-alcoholic version of essence.

vinegar

balsamic originally from Modena, Italy, there are now many balsamic vinegars on the market ranging in quality and pungency depending on how long they have been aged; use the most expensive sparingly.

red wine made from rice wine lees (sediment), salt and alcohol.

worcestershire a thin, dark-brown, spicy sauce used as a seasoning for meat, gravies and cocktails, and as a condiment.

zucchini also known as courgette; small pale- or dark-green, yellow or white members of the squash family having edible flowers that can be stuffed and deep-fried or oven-baked.

conversion chart

MEASURES

One Australian metric measuring cup holds approximately 250ml, one Australian metric tablespoon holds 20ml, one Australian metric teaspoon holds 5ml.

The difference between one country's measuring cups and another's is within a 2- or 3-teaspoon variance, and will not affect your cooking results. North America, New Zealand and the United Kingdom use a 15ml tablespoon. All cup and spoon measurements are level. The most accurate way of measuring dry ingredients is to weigh them. When measuring liquids, use a clear glass or plastic jug with metric markings.

We use large eggs with an average weight of 60g.

DRY MEASURES

METRIC	IMPERIAL
15g	½oz
30g	1oz
60g	2oz
90g	3oz
125g	4oz (¼lb)
155g	5oz
185g	6oz
220g	7oz
250g	8oz (½lb)
280g	9oz
315g	10oz
345g	11oz
375g	12oz (¾lb)
410g	13oz
440g	14oz
470g	15oz
500g	16oz (1lb)
750g	24oz (1½lb)
1kg	32oz (2lb)

LIQUID MEASURES

METRIC	IMPERIAL
30ml	1 fluid oz
60ml	2 fluid oz
100ml	3 fluid oz
125ml	4 fluid oz
150ml	5 fluid oz (¼ pint/1 gill)
190ml	6 fluid oz
250ml	8 fluid oz
300ml	10 fluid oz (½ pint)
500ml	16 fluid oz
600ml	20 fluid oz (1 pint)
1000ml (1 litre)	1¾ pints

LENGTH MEASURES

METRIC	IMPERIAL
3mm	⅛in
6mm	¼in
1cm	½in
2cm	¾in
2.5cm	1in
5cm	2in
6cm	2½in
8cm	3in
10cm	4in
13cm	5in
15cm	6in
18cm	7in
20cm	8in
23cm	9in
25cm	10in
28cm	11in
30cm	12in (1ft)

OVEN TEMPERATURES

These oven temperatures are only a guide for conventional ovens. For fan-forced ovens, check the manufacturer's manual.

	°C (CELSIUS)	°F (FAHRENHEIT)	GAS MARK
Very slow	120	250	½
Slow	150	275 – 300	1 – 2
Moderately slow	160	325	3
Moderate	180	350 – 375	4 – 5
Moderately hot	200	400	6
Hot	220	425 – 450	7 – 8
Very hot	240	475	9

index

A
anchovy and onion tartlets 13
antipasto puff pastry tartlets 14
apple and blackberry pie 34
apple tart, caramelised 50
avocado salsa 17

B
bacon, rocket and
   potato frittata 5
beetroot and caramelised
   onion tart 6
blackberry and apple pie 34
butterscotch chocolate
   tartlets 25

C
caramel chocolate tarts 46
caramelised apple tart 50
caramelised onion and
   beetroot tart 6
caramelised onion tart 10
chive oil 6
chocolate butterscotch
   tartlets 25
chocolate caramel tarts 46
chocolate cases with
   mascarpone and berries 58
chocolate jaffa tart 42
chocolate ricotta tart 49
chocolate tart, rich 29
corn cake with salsa, creamy 17
cottage pies 2
creamy corn cake with salsa 17
crème fraîche sauce 9
crème pâtissière 33

F
fillings
   lemon 54
   lime 41
   pecan, macadamia
      and walnut 45
   ricotta 49

frittata, rocket, potato
   and bacon 5
fudge sauce, hot 38

G
galette, rhubarb 53
galette, peach 57

H
horseradish cream 6
hot fudge sauce 38

I
ice-cream pie, peanut butter
   and fudge 38

L
lemon filling 54
lemon tart 54
lime filling 41
lime macaroon tart 41
lime meringue pie 26
lime meringue tartlets 22

M
macaroon topping 41
mini pecan, macadamia
   and walnut pies 45

N
nectarine tart, roast 33

O
oil, chive 6
onion and anchovy tartlets 13
onion and beetroot
   tart, caramelised 6
onion tart, caramelised 10

P
pastry
   blackberry and apple pie 34
   pear tarte tatin 21
   pecan pie 30
   prune and custard tart 18
   rich chocolate tart 29
   roast nectarine tart 33
   tarte tatin 37

peach galette 57
peanut butter and fudge
   ice-cream pie 38
pear tarte tatin 21
pecan pie 30
pecan, macadamia and
   walnut pies, mini 45
pesto, traditional 10
pie, blackberry and apple 34
pie, lime meringue 26
pie, peanut butter and
   fudge ice-cream 38
pie, pecan 30
pies, cottage 2
pies, mini pecan, macadamia
   and walnut 45
potato, rocket and
   bacon frittata 5
prune and custard tart 18

R
rhubarb galette 53
ricotta filling 49

S
salsa, avocado 17
sauce, crème fraîche 9
sauce, hot fudge 38

T
tarte tatin 37
tarte tatin, pear 21
tarte tatins, tomato, with
   crème fraîche sauce 9
tartlets, antipasto puff pastry 14
tartlets, chocolate
   butterscotch 25
tartlets, lime meringue 22
tartlets, onion and anchovy 13
tarts, caramel chocolate 46
tomato tarte tatins with crème
   fraîche sauce 9
topping, macaroon 41
traditional pesto 10

Are you missing some of the world's favourite cookbooks?

The Australian Women's Weekly cookbooks are available from bookshops, cookshops, supermarkets and other stores all over the world. You can also buy direct from the publisher, using the order form below.

MINI SERIES £3.50 190x138MM 64 PAGES

TITLE	QTY	TITLE	QTY	TITLE	QTY
4 Fast Ingredients		Finger Food		Salads	
15-minute Feasts		Gluten-free Cooking		Simple Slices	
50 Fast Chicken Fillets		Healthy Everyday Food 4 Kids		Simply Seafood	
50 Fast Desserts		Ice-creams & Sorbets		Skinny Food	
After-work Stir-fries		Indian Cooking		Spanish Favourites	
Barbecue Chicken		Indonesian Favourites		Stir-fries	
Biscuits, Brownies & Biscotti		Italian Favourites		Summer Salads	
Bites		Jams & Jellies		Tagines & Couscous	
Bowl Food		Japanese Favourites		Tapas, Antipasto & Mezze	
Burgers, Rösti & Fritters		Kids Party Food		Tarts	
Cafe Cakes		Last-minute Meals		Tex-Mex (May 07)	
Cafe Food		Lebanese Cooking		Thai Favourites	
Casseroles		Low-Fat Delicious		The Fast Egg	
Casseroles & Curries		Low Fat Fast		The Packed Lunch	
Char-grills & Barbecues		Malaysian Favourites		Vegetarian	
Cheesecakes, Pavlova & Trifles		Mince		Vegie Main Meals	
Chinese Favourites		Mince Favourites		Vietnamese Favourites	
Chocolate Cakes		Muffins		Wok	
Christmas Cakes & Puddings		Noodles		Young Chef	
Cocktails		Outdoor Eating			
Crumbles & Bakes		Party Food			
Curries		Pickles and Chutneys			
Dried Fruit & Nuts		Pasta			
Drinks		Potatoes			
Fast Soup		Roast		TOTAL COST	£

Photocopy and complete coupon below

Name _____

Address _____

_____ Postcode _____

Country _____ Phone (business hours) _____

Email*(optional) _____
*By including your email address, you consent to receipt of any email regarding this magazine, and other emails which inform you of ACP's other publications, products, services and events, and to promote third party goods and services you may be interested in.

I enclose my cheque/money order for £ _____ or please charge £ _____

to my: ☐ Access ☐ Mastercard ☐ Visa ☐ Diners Club
PLEASE NOTE: WE DO NOT ACCEPT SWITCH OR ELECTRON CARDS

Card number | | | | | | | | | | | | | | | | |

3 digit security code *(found on reverse of card)* _____

Cardholder's
signature _____ Expiry date ____ /____

To order: Mail or fax – photocopy or complete the order form above, and send your credit card details or cheque payable to: Australian Consolidated Press (UK), 10 Scirocco Close, Moulton Park Office Village, Northampton NN3 6AP, phone (+44) (01) 604 642200, fax (+44) (01) 604 642300, fax (+44) (01) 604 497533, e-mail books@acpuk.com or order online at www.acpuk.com.
Non-UK residents: We accept the credit cards listed on the coupon, or cheques, drafts or International Money Orders payable in sterling and drawn on a UK bank. Credit card charges are at the exchange rate current at the time of payment.
All pricing current at time of going to press and subject to change/availability.
Postage and packing UK: Add £1.00 per order plus 25p per book.
Postage and packing overseas: Add £2.00 per order plus 50p per book. **Offer ends 31.12.2007**